# THE UNCHANGING HOPI

# THE UNCHANGING HOPI

*An Artist's Interpretation in Scratchboard Drawings and Text*

BY BARTON WRIGHT

With a Foreword by Bruce E. Babbitt

NORTHLAND PRESS

SECOND PRINTING — JUNE, 1976

ISBN 0–87358–118–0
Library of Congress Catalog Card Number 74–31543
Composed and Printed in the United States of America

To Clay Lockett

# *Contents*

# *Foreword*

TWO HUNDRED YEARS AGO, while rebellious British colonials were circulating a declaration of independence in Philadelphia, Spain was still trying to convert and civilize the Hopi Indians. On July 4, 1776, while the fires of liberty blazed in the American colonies, an adventurous missionary priest named Francisco Garcés, rode into the Great Plaza at Oraibi to again beseech the Hopis to hear his message of salvation. The Hopis were unmoved; they remained sullen and refused his gifts. After a lonely night in the Plaza, Garcés rode back to Tucson.

Three months later, in September, 1776, another wandering Franciscan missionary, Silvestre Vélez de Escalante, entered the Hopi villages on his way back to Santa Fe from a long journey of exploration and discovery. The Hopis were a little more friendly, but they absolutely refused to hear any preaching.

A few decades later Spain's empire in North America melted away, leaving the fruits of centuries of conflict with the Pueblo Indians. For the Hopis the fruit was mostly bitter, expressed in dark tales of the great pueblo revolt in 1680, the massacre of Spanish priests and soldiers, the fratricidal razing of Awatovi, use of forced labor to drag mountain timber from miles away to build churches, priestly abuse of Hopi women and disruption of sacred ceremonials. Today the only tangible remains of Spanish domination are the dwarf peach trees rooted in sandy hillsides and horses and sheep grazing on plains below the pueblos.

A mere hundred years ago, the American age that began in Philadelphia finally reached the Hopi mesas. Manifest destiny came to northern Arizona on iron rails, bringing successive waves of traders, government officials, tourists, anthropologists — and more missionaries. The Americans came to stay, and they have printed their mark more indelibly in a hundred years than Spain did in three centuries.

Today, on the eve of the American Bicentennial, many students and admirers of Hopi culture are again asking whether this complex, profound and resilient civilization will continue to flourish or whether it is doomed to extinction, going the way of the Mandans, the Comanches, and a hundred other Indian tribes. Could it be that Barton Wright's sketches will someday be viewed as documents of a vanished people just as are Catlin's sketches of the Mandans and Curtis' photographs of the Comanches?

Barton Wright, and a handful of others like him, are out to make certain that their studies do not become historic relics of a vanished culture. As curator of the Museum of Northern Arizona, he prepares the annual Hopi Craftsman Show which has set standards of excellence and created increasing demand for traditional Hopi crafts. In his previous book, *Kachinas: A Hopi Artist's Documentary,* Wright's contribution to the Hopi record is quite significant. His writing and the paintings by Cliff Bahnimptewa, a Hopi artist, take up where Jesse Walter Fewkes and an earlier generation of Hopi artists left the subject in 1900.

In this book Wright's scratchboards take me back to a subzero February night on Second Mesa, waiting to climb down into a warm kiva to be hypnotized by the rhythmic chanting motion of the kachinas, to a crowded plaza on a hot July day as the Niman Kachinas prepare to leave, and to hours spent conversing with Hopi elders across time and two cultures. For those who haven't been to the Hopi villages, these sketches are not the stuff of fantasy; they are pure, true distillations of a culture steeped in tradition, living in harmony with the natural order and responsive to a profound spiritual belief.

Barton Wright, by deed and by pen, is building bridges between cultures. If enough of us can occasionally cross those bridges to see and comprehend, perhaps both the Hopis and their neighbors will still be around to celebrate an American Tricentennial.

BRUCE E. BABBITT
*Attorney General of Arizona*

# *Introduction*

TO CALL THE HOPI UNCHANGING is in truth not correct for they are changing as inexorably as any other race. Their apparent timelessness springs equally from the ageless quality of their villages and surroundings and from their slower tempo of living. With today's spate of ephemerae and the rush and surge of "progress" toward an ill-defined goal there lies within most of us a wistful desire for a modicum of permanence or simplicity. The Hopi clinging to an older order and hoarding his values in the face of this flood give a transient appearance of permanence.

This appearance has made the Hopi more and more of a lodestone attracting alike those who would in some flight of personal fantasy "return to nature" as well as the sincerely interested humanitarian and the gamut between. The Hopis, defensively, have achieved the admirable quality of one-way glass, casually reflecting for the intruder's edification his own images and desires, while they continue their own activities behind this successful screen. They live within guidelines laid down by preceding generations, and the weight of this tradition continues to dictate clan relationships, ritual behavior, social position and political decisions even today. Without this inbred knowledge, the Hopis are but dimly perceived. The first-time visitor is overwhelmed by strong impressions. The neutral blending tones of mesa and house heighten to unexpected intensity the blaze of color in a kachina dance. Surprise at the sophistication of these warm hospitable people conflicts with astonishment at the incredible clutter of an inadequate garbage disposal. An outsider is assaulted by all of the attributes of any small town, compressed and intensified until, in his bemusement, the visitor seizes upon his own predilections as characteristic of the Hopis.

The mirror of my own association with Hopis reflects a constant wonder at the absoluteness of contrasts, such as their ability to stand rock solid in their tradition, and yet slip easily into the rush of our society. Through a somewhat unconscious process, scratchboard became to me the medium most suitable to catch this attribute of the Hopis. The starkness of black and white epitomized both their contrasts as well as the duality of their basic concepts. For Hopi thought divides the universe between those living in a plane of light, weight and mass, with their creative deity, the Sun, picking out the extremes of light and shadow, and the mist-like dead existing in their land of darkness, spirits and insubstantiality presided over by a deity of fire, death and darkness. This concept of duality permeates every aspect of Hopi thought and action and in my own mind became linked with the attributes of scratchboard.

Scratchboard is not a well known media today although the technique has been used by artists throughout the world to achieve certain effects for thousands of years. Indeed the earliest art in the Southwest used precisely the same technique except that a sharp rock was used to cut through the desert varnish on some cliff side and expose the lighter rock beneath. Centuries later the inhabitants of the ruined village of Awatovi used this same technique to execute designs on their pottery.

Quite simply scratchboard is a good grade of cardboard coated with an inert pigment. This substance is clay, usually kaolin or whiting, bound with a glue or casein size in correct amounts to produce a ground or gesso on the board. The resulting board will take India ink on the surface yet allow the artist to cut or scrape through the coating thereby removing portions of the ink and leaving a white line. Referred to in many artist's manuals in faintly derogatory terms as a media for advertising art, it is one of the lesser used techniques. The quality of line which can be produced is not easily duplicated by pen or brush, and a free, loose style is as easy to achieve as the rigidity of a technical illustration. The effects range from a very close imitation of a wood cut or wood engraving to one similar to an etching.

# *The Unchanging Hopi*

# *Origins and Migrations*

## THE GRAND CANYON

The Grand Canyon is a place of awe for the Hopis because deep in the bottom of the gorge is the original *sipapu,* the mystic opening joining the two worlds of the quick and the dead. The Hopis believe that they emerged from the Underworld at this sacred place. Mythically the dying Hopis return to this chasm as wisps of vapor drifting downward into the canyon on their return to the Underworld. The Hopis who formerly ventured to the bottom of the canyon to bring back salt (a deposit forms close by the *sipapu*) returned with eerie tales. If one passed just before rounding the last bend to the *sipapu,* laughter and singing of happy people could be heard. However, as one approached it the voices faded away and only the sound of the river remained.

The ancestral Hopis formerly occupied the so-called "Strip" country which lies between the border of Utah and the North Rim of the Grand Canyon. Along the Colorado River from the Crossing of the Fathers to the Grand Wash Cliffs, virtually the only sure crossing of the river lies next to the *sipapu.*

B.Wright

## INSCRIPTION HOUSE

Long before most of the Hopi pueblos were established some of the people occupied the deep red sandstone canyons to the north. Such a habitation is Inscription House, hugging its narrow ledge high in the canyon wall. The people who lived here and planted the canyon floor were gone for centuries when archaeologists visited it, scratching about in their abandoned rooms and refuse heaps. In one such room the archaeologists discovered a dim inscription on the wall, presumably in Spanish, which they believed to date from Escalante's trip through this wilderness in 1776. The fact that it was made by Mormon explorers scarcely one hundred years before did not become known until a decade or so after it had been set aside as a national monument.

## WUPATKI

The Hopi believe that in the bottom of the Grand Canyon lies the original *sipapu,* the opening through which they emerged into this world. Journeying slowly southward from the *sipapu* the clans would pause at likely locations to settle, sometimes for a lengthy period or again for a short time. Here they would plant their seed corn to replenish their supplies. One frequently mentioned location in many of the clan stories is Wupatki, located northeast of the San Francisco Peaks, dotted with abandoned villages both large and small. Today the summer rains drift over these long deserted ruins leaving behind the green of growing plants much as did the perennially moving Hopis centuries ago.

B. Wright

## NUVATIKYAOVI

Receiving different names from every surrounding Indian tribe, passing Spaniard, and exploring American, the San Francisco Peaks demand attention. They dominate every horizon for hundreds of miles. The snows that mantle their slopes lend a mirage-like image of clouds to the winter skies. Enormous thunderheads fling their banners first from the tips of these peaks in deep summer. Small wonder that all surrounding tribes refer to them as the place where the snow abides and attribute to them a holiness. For the Hopis it is the home of many of their rain-bringing supernaturals, the kachinas, and the abode of a storm deity. That this is so is obvious for rain begins first on their slopes and moisture is always present. The deep green of spruce, symbol of abundant crops, shows there. When placing prayer feathers high on these slopes or gathering spruce for a ceremony the voices of the kachinas are audible to the visiting Hopi.

BWright

## MIGRATION

The Hopis, bound to their mesa tops today by encroaching enemies and government proscriptions, were not always so sedentary. Their history is one of coming and going over the land. Mingling and separating, planting their crops, holding ceremonies, occasionally fighting, they eddied about from river to mountain to mesa, drawn always by a bright promise of better things whispered to them by their clan kachinas. Led by the interpretations and dreams of their wise old men and protected by the strength of their young men, they moved as a village from one favored location to another, leaving behind the cast-off shell of their living for the delight of future archaeologists.

## MISHONGNOVI

Mishongnovi is old in its present setting even though it has moved more than once to reach this location. Long ago when the disrupting Spanish first appeared, Mishongnovi lay at the foot of the cliff below Koyashtoro. It had occupied this area after its inhabitants fled from Köngoivi with its mythical child-destroying monster. Constricted by the mesa top where it is today, it grew to an imposing height by the beginning of this century. Long rows of rooms tiered one above the other rose as many as four stories in height with clean plastered exteriors. Roofs of the lower houses were used by the upstairs neighbors as handy work areas or preferred spots from which to watch the dances in the plazas below. Then as the new century began the people began to drift slowly to the surrounding off-reservation towns and down the slopes of the mesa to cluster at its base. Old Mishongnovi shrank, a room here and roof there, until the tall houses had disappeared leaving only the lower rooms.

## THE PAIUTE

The Paiutes, distant Shoshone cousins, lived on the juniper-covered stretches of the Kaibeto Plateau to the north of the Hopis. Historically a mild-mannered people, they were usually on friendly terms with their neighbors and given to visiting when the weather was right for a little sightseeing and trading or a bit of wrestling. Frequently some dignified Hopi intent upon a trading deal with a Paiute would find himself being set upon by his overeager visitor and wrestled about. The sunshade was an identifying characteristic of the Paiutes as they came jogging along over the barren rocks and hot sandy slopes to visit. This improvised parasol was made of cottonwood shoots thrust into the hair and tied to shade head and shoulders from the hot sun. Seen from a distance they often resembled small bushy green trees moving across the valley floor as they approached the Hopi villages.

B. Wright

## WALPI

Undoubtedly the most picturesque of all Hopi towns, Walpi has been captured on canvas or film by countless individuals. To each visitor it offers an array of vistas or vignettes to snare his imagination and try his skills. Today, though photography of the dwindling village is prohibited, visitors in ever-increasing numbers make their way to its door. The people of Walpi regard this horde with mixed feelings for it is a potential menace given to stealing photographs and transgressing in unguessed ways, and yet it is an active market for their crafts. In spite of this interest the village continues its slow passage down the road to final ruin. Each year sees inexorable change in the old village. A house collapses or is abandoned, a road is introduced or a wall of stone disappears to be replaced with chicken wire. The encroaching glare of carbon arcs and incandescence in the neighboring villages now threaten to banish forever the shadows of the night and the past from this old town.

## A DIFFERENT TEACHER

The Navajos are the neighbors of the Hopis and have been for generations. They drifted into the same area as the Hopis at least three hundred years ago. However, the mores and concepts of the two cultures are so widely variant that they have been mutual irritants ever since. Individually they have been friends, relatives, in-laws, wives and husbands or adopted children, but collectively they are enemies. The Hopis make mock of the Navajos in subtle ways, portraying them as clowns for amusement in their various dances. Yet they perform the Tasap Kachina, a Navajo inspired supernatural, for one of their most sacred ceremonies. The far-ranging Navajos will take unmerciful advantage of land and livestock belonging to their more peaceful town-dwelling neighbors and yet often marry and settle down in one of the villages. Present land disputes are simply a continuation of generations of friction between neighbors, and it is very doubtful if this can be settled by fiat of a legislative body.

*The People*

## TAWAQUOPTEWA

Undoubtedly Tawaquoptewa, the leader of Old Oraibi, was one of the most well known Hopi of the past generation. It was he who reaped the whirlwind of dissension following the division of Oraibi at the turn of the century. Impaled by governmental edicts that could not be resolved by Hopi standards, he was jailed at Alcatraz, ridiculed and abandoned by his fellow Hopis. In his declining years his attempts to initiate assistance from non-governmental whites brought him the role of a quaint old character who carved weird kachina dolls rather than the aid and position he so desperately wanted. He died acquainted with thousands, yet unknown except to a few.

B Wright

## THE CHAKMONGWI

From ancient times there was formerly a man in all Hopi towns who was the talking chief or *chakmongwi*. It was this person's duty to call out messages to the passing Cloud People. Climbing atop a particular building he would address these spirit people about the most important occasions with messages specifically for them. However, any of the villagers could also listen if they so desired. In recent years the position has fallen into disuse with the disintegrating ceremonial life of the Hopis. No longer do the Cloud People hear the bell-like chant of the *chakmongwi's* voice echoing over a peaceful village on some still desert morning.

B. Wright

## THE MAN OF STATURE

This Hopi man was a man of great stature among his people. While many of the things he did would not seem remarkable to non-Hopis, he was revered for his service and wisdom. As a young man he was strikingly handsome, and with age his face took on dignity and registered his inner strength and character. He was widely known both in his own village and throughout the Southwest and was well liked. His forceful presence could usually be found in the vanguard of the active participants of village or tribal efforts. During dance days his home on the plaza was filled to bursting by both Indian and non-Indian visitors, most of whom were fed as well as offered sitting room. While he did not hold a chief's rank in the village hierarchy, very often it was he who furnished leadership when it was needed or balance when personalities clashed.

BWright

## THE MAIDEN

One of the most time-consuming yet becoming hairstyles was that of the young Hopi maiden. Symbolically their hair represented either the squash blossom or the wings of a butterfly with all the implications of the promise of new life. Turn of the century visitors brought back countless photographs of serene young women with shining black hair done in butterfly headdresses. Set off by maiden shawls of scarlet, black and white and gaily fringed Portugese shawls, they were posed on walls and steps, by cliff and spring until the impact reached through the black and white photography of earlier days to bring us the sensation of their colorful beauty.

B Wright

## THE HOPI WOMAN

The root of the Hopi village is the clan grandmother. Men may roam about, work the fields or hold their religious ceremonies, but it is the clan matriarch, forever at home, who is the real power. She controls lives through the branching lines of female descendants and the land through their husbands and sons. She is the caretaker of the most sacred religious objects, a director of thought and a participant of many ceremonies. She is the ultimate conservative, the cohesive focus of the Hopis and their way of life.

## THE HOPI MAN

The older Hopi man sits as solidly in his environment as a rock in a wall. His ethic is one of closeness to the earth and the natural forces which surround him. His unhurried passage through life gives him time for thought and humor and an innate politeness and hospitality frequently forgotten by "busy" people. His work is tied to the earth, his food acquired through the strength of his religion, his amusement by cooperation with neighbors and his everyday needs by the deftness of his hands. The satisfaction of this life adds the lines of dignity and humor to the faces of older Hopi men.

B.Wright

## HAIR DRESSING

The Hopi women dress their men's hair in this fashion even today. The clothing and seating has changed but not the method. The older men particularly, but also the younger ones who are returning to long hair, have it dressed in this manner. The brush being used is the all-purpose grass bundle tied so one end is short and can be used for grooming their hair. The long end is used as a broom. The men's hair is divided into a bang that hangs over the eyes. The side locks are trimmed even with the angle of the jaw and hang in dutch boy style. The back hair is gathered and caught in the center with a wool cord and tied into a small vertical bow or knot. This particular scene was adapted from an historic photograph.

## THE SPINNER

The Hopi men still weave wedding robes, sashes, dresses, kilts and a couple of kinds of belts. While string has unfortunately been taken over as the warp element in their weaving, the weft is generally of hand-spun wool or cotton. To make the wool or cotton yarn for their weaving is an arduous task that requires hours of carding, then spinning with a hand-held spindle that is rolled along the thigh to give the yarn a twist. After its initial spinning the yarn has a tendency to be lumpy and uneven. This is smoothed by holding the spindle whorl under one foot, grasping the yarn with either hand and carefully pulling the lumps out as a Hopi is doing in this version of an historic photograph. The Hopis did not consider this an important task but rather referred to it as *tamala,* busy work, the sort of thing to be done when one is resting from more important jobs.

BWright

## THE MAIDEN WHORL

Long ago all young unmarried women wore their hair in so-called butterfly whorls. These bouffant puffs of hair at either side of the head were felt to resemble the wings of butterflies and represent by association spring, the rebirth of life and beauty. A second person and a good deal of time were required to keep a girl's hair in this form. The hair was drawn to either side and wound about a U-shaped piece of wood. It was then caught and tied in the exact center of the U and between the wooden frame and the head. The hair frame or *nasömñoila* was then withdrawn and the hair puffed out. If the girl had an abundance of hair the whorls tended to droop during the day, often giving them the appearance of horns rather than the desired shape. In recent years this beautiful hairstyle has been relegated to only the most special occasions for no one seems to have the time nor the desire to fashion it thus.

B Wright

## THE HOPI HAT

Today the mark of the conservative Hopi is the brilliant kerchief knotted about his head with the ends fluttering in the breeze. Yet this kerchief is a comparatively recent addition to his dress for at the turn of the century only a few of the men wore them. The remainder went bareheaded or wore cowboy hats. Nowadays after a long interval of almost universal wear, the gaiety of prints and the expansive choices of color are disappearing, and only those who dress for an occasion or the conservative older men choose to wear the colorful "Hopi hat."

BWright

Ceremonies

## THE SHRINE

At the winter solstice the Hopis hold a ceremony known as the Soyalunga. In the kivas the men ceremonially turn the sun back toward the path of summer. Additionally for the coming day they make *pahos* or prayer carriers from bits of willow stems and feathers. Long before dawn the men move through the village presenting relatives and friends with *pahos* that symbolize their wishes for a good new year. *Pahos* are placed on fruit trees and animals that they may increase and on houses that they may be sturdy until the entire village is bedecked with these visible prayers. The final rite is held just as the sun appears over the horizon. The women make their way to their shrine to ask for long life and good health. The men go to another and as they sprinkle corn meal toward the rising sun, ask to be good providers and for a long and productive life.

B. Wright

## THE RETURNING SUN

Soyal is the Hopi New Year. It is a time for renewal and strengthening of the world and all of its aspects. It is a time for prayers for relatives, friends and neighbors and their well-being. Blessings are asked for the forthcoming crops in the approaching season of growth and for an increase of animals. Most particularly, kachinas appear to bless and strengthen the village and the important clan houses. On Second Mesa, Ahöla and Ahöl Mana, his "sister," arrive and make their way from one important location to another, marking and blessing each. Despite the snow and bitter cold or frigid winds that so often mark this time of year on the mesas, the two kachinas pass through the village on their appointed rounds, heralds of the returning sun of another year.

BWright 75

## THE KIVA DANCE

In a Hopi village, all homes are owned by the women. Kivas are the only structures which belong to the men. Hopi men are responsible for the religious life of their people, and a kiva, the entrance to the spirit world, is the place from which ceremonies emanate. In the cold months after the winter solstice the kachinas appear and dance at night in the kivas. These underground ceremonial chambers are havens of light and warmth in a frigid world where the audience dozes on the banquettes awaiting the arrival of the kachinas. All of the kivas put forth a group of dancers and each group must dance at least once and often twice in every kiva in the village. Usually there are at least four kivas, and the dancers drift ghost-like through the star-lit streets and biting cold to a kiva. Casting off blankets or coats if they have deigned to wear them, they announce their presence with a stamp or a call. With the shouted welcome of the kiva chief from below, they descend the ladder into the lighted chamber. Their entry and dance transforms the kiva into a theater of movement and color for the excited audience.

B.Wright

## THE DANCER

The men who come to dance at the kivas during the cold wintry months of January and February are of every age. If the dance requires women, these parts are assumed by the men and boys. Preparation for the dance is in their own kiva, and here the scene is the equivalent of the backstage in any theatre. Painting, dressing, affixing each other's feathers and checking last minute details, they ready themselves for the performance. Standing about the kiva many of the handsome younger men who are dressed as women appear as beautiful as the girls they portray. Then with a swing of shoulders, long stride or swaggering step they completely destroy the illusion.

BWright

## THE VIGIL

The early morning arrival of the Niman Kachinas on their last visit of the year is always watched by some of the villagers. Mounting to the rooftops, they stand in the crisp morning air wrapped in shawls or blankets, patiently awaiting the kachinas' arrival and their meeting with the elders at the kiva. In the strong cross light of the morning the watchers stand and sit as motionless as the chimneys that besprinkle the flat-topped roofs of town.

## THE DANCE PLAZA

In every Hopi village there is an open area that is available for dancing or ceremonies. The picturesque plaza at Walpi with its peculiar rock formation is undoubtedly one of the most photographed locations in Hopi territory. Countless photographers have recorded Snake dances, Flute ceremonies and other events until in desperation the Hopi denied all visitors the right to film anything. The dun-colored backdrop of houses and plaza makes the sunlight appear more intense and the color of the audience and the performers' clothes stand out as brilliant flares of color. This, as well as the other-worldliness of the dances, creates an irresistible need to record a memorable event.

BWright

## NIMAN MORNING

In July the kachinas visit the Hopis for the last time and then return to their homes on the peaks and in springs at the rim of the Hopi world. They dance one last day and disappear with the exception of a few of the most important who appear the following morning for a brief ceremony to close the kivas to kachinas for another year. They are met by the Hopi chiefs at their respective kivas. In the strong clear light of the early morning the final ceremony begins with a mere handful of onlookers, the faithful and the curious as witnesses.

## THE RACE

When the coolness of fall hangs over the mesa country and the Hopis have harvested their crops, the time comes for the women's ceremonials. While the women prepare to dance in the clear, bright sunlight of the plazas, the men race to receive the prizes they offer. Most of the males in the village, regardless of age, enter these contests of endurance. There are several races, all during the late summer and fall and all associated with the women's basket dances. Never a short distance, the race of today is short compared to that of yesteryear. A three-mile sprint along the level reaches of sage and sand only limbers up the young men for the final race of ten miles or more which is climaxed by a rush up the six hundred foot flanks of the mesa.

BWright

## THE BUTTERFLY DANCE

Many of the Hopi dances have originated among the Eastern Pueblos along the Rio Grande and have been traded and borrowed from tribe to tribe in the manner of any commodity. Some dances are changed sufficiently that the instigators no longer recognize their own devising and borrow them back. One of the most popular and widespread of all dances is the Butterfly which is performed by virtually all pueblos. It is curiously oriental in economy of gesture and very graceful in the precision of movement. Because the Butterfly Dance is a social performance rather than a religious rite it is quite often presented at Powwows or other Indian gatherings. This particular dancer is from a Rio Grande pueblo. In appearance she differs from a Hopi Butterfly Dancer only in hairstyle.

B Wright

# *Kachinas and Dances*

## THE UNDERWORLD

Kivas are places of mystery and drama at night. The light emerges from below, and figures of men and kachinas passing through it assume heroic proportions by its reversed glow. Kachinas rising along the ladders of the kivas become believable as other-world beings briefly visiting the villages of the Hopi. These coupled with the shadowy figures of onlookers coalescing, drifting apart, knotting again lend a Dantean quality to the scene. The belief slowly grips the visitor that a doorway to the Underworld has been opened and figures are passing freely to and fro between the two worlds of spirit and mass.

B Wright

## THE CORN GIRL

On First Mesa at the beginning of the kachina season, three kachinas appear to perform their duties. Ahul, the leader, ceremonially greets the returning sun as it rises. Near him stands the Yellow Corn Girl, Kachin Mana and the Blue Corn Girl, Sakwap Mana. Each is bearing a basket tray in which the colored ears of corn are set vertically around a core of packed cotton and the entirety surrounded by green spruce boughs, a visual representation of the prayers of the village. As Ahul roars out his cryptic message to the sun and as the Corn Girls present their burdens in view of the sun, the year begins.

BWright '75

## ANGWUSHAHAI-I — THE CROW BRIDE

Only at Hotevilla in February is it possible to see this stately figure, for she never appeared at the other villages and comes no longer to Oraibi. The Crow Bride appears far away from the village at first light and begins her journey to the town. As she advances she pauses at prescribed intervals to stand and sing until at last she enters the plaza just as the sun breaks the horizon. In her hands she carries a tray filled with seeds and corn sprouts. Quietly the women of the village approach the kachina as she stands and sings. They take a few of the seeds, casting cornmeal to her in thanks. Angwushahai-i never breaks her slow considered advance toward a particular kiva. She pauses at the kiva until the chiefs emerge, remove the remainder of her gift and sprinkle her with meal. Turning, Angwushahai-i continues her solemn way toward the San Francisco Peaks and disappears from view.

B Wright

## THE PRESENT BRINGER

In February the Hopis have an important ceremony that symbolizes the approaching spring and the renewal of the world. Qöqöle kachinas arrive and bring the Hopis samples of the new crops. The appearance of delicate new bean sprouts in the hands of kachinas when all about lies snow and ice is indeed proof of their supernatural abilities, though the children do not know the beans were raised in the kivas. Hanging from the bean sprouts in the hands of the kachinas are moccasins, rattles, bows and arrows and dolls for the Hopi children. The most favored of all the kachinas who appear at sunrise during the Powamu (Bean Dance) are the Qöqölom. Carrying large baskets on their backs and dressed in long buckskin robes they mutter to themselves as they bob about through the village bringing presents to the children who await this Hopi Santa Claus on every doorstep and street corner.

## THE NIGHT DANCE

Many of the kivas present an appearance of great antiquity regardless of their age. Looking at one of these buildings in the dark of a Hopi night is similar to standing among the ruins of a long deserted village. Rocks lie tumbled about in partial disarray, poles protrude at awkward angles, debris lays about as though the inhabitants had departed long ago. Suddenly a dim glow of light will illuminate a portion of the kiva and nightmarish shapes pour out the top and down the sides like a freshly disturbed ant hill. The silhouetted or partially lit kachinas swarm about, then cluster and move off into total darkness, leaving one with the impression that it was an afterimage of an event that happened in times long past.

B Wright

## THE CORN DANCERS

The Corn Kachinas are dancing a call to the spirit world to aid them in growing corn to feed themselves and their families. The Corn Kachinas will bring the rain to grow the corn, the strength for the plant to resist the insects or diseases that may attack it and the essence of corn necessary for it to mature to its fullest. The Corn Kachinas always wear headdresses of four feathers radiating to the four directions and in this dance at Bakabi they were particularly noticeable. The sun was in the west and the wind had blown a sheet of ocherish dust over the entire sky. The audience along the roof tops were silhouettes with almost no color while the reflected light in the plaza outlined the kachina dancers and picked out the highlights of their bodies and the feathers they wore. Despite weeping eyes from the blowing dust and the attempt of the wind to strip the clothing from your body it was a beautiful dance.

B. Wright

## ANGWUSI—THE CROW

Clowns perform in the plaza during intervals in the spring dances when the kachinas leave to rest. Their antics are frequently risqué but always comic and ever more boisterous and daring as the day advances. Any and all activities of the Hopis are burlesqued, to the amusement of the crowd. Gradually however the audience becomes aware of other kachinas that stand menacingly armed at the plaza corners. They may be an ogre or a bird such as an owl or crow who momentarily appears and then vanishes. But at each pause in the dance they stay longer and advance more aggressively toward the clowns. At the close of the day these warriors descend en masse upon the hapless clowns and punish them unmercifully for their transgressions during the day.

B Wright

## THE KACHINKI

When the kachinas dance in the village plazas they do so in a series of performances. Each performance consists of dancing on each of the four sides of the plaza and then retiring for a short while to rest before repeating the performance. They may dance as many as sixteen sets during the course of a day. The dance is done by standing on one leg and stamping out a rhythm with the other foot. Between each performance the kachinas pass in single file from the plaza to the mesa edge and over to the *kachinki* or kachina's home to rest. Here the kiva chiefs and sponsors sit and smoke, meditating on their prayers to the spirits for rain. The weary dancers push aside their masks to cool their brows and sit or stand about, resting. Nowadays all visitors are barred from the *kachinki,* although formerly non-Indians were not barred unless they overstepped the bounds of hospitality.

## THE NIMAN KACHINA

The last dance of the kachinas for six months is the Niman, when all of them return home after the summer solstice. Usually the Niman is performed by the Hemis Kachina with Kachin Manas although others can appear. During the pause between dances, the kachinas stride about the plaza in their towering headgear, their arms loaded with entire corn plants and an occasional cattail. Tied to these plants at mid point is a present for some youngster. The plaza becomes a sea of green as more and more corn plants are delivered among the audience. The children rush about with their loads of greenery to drop them in their mothers' laps as they bear away their presents.

B. Wright

# *Myths and Legends*

## THE OLD VILLAGE

Characteristic of the older sections of most Hopi villages is the area along the road into Mishongnovi. The strata of the mesa top merge so gradually into the walls of structures that the houses appear a result of rock weathering rather than human effort. The fractured rock of the cliff becomes the carefully laid rock until the village appears to grow from the very earth. When you are at this place, it is not difficult to be empathetic with the Hopi belief that villages grow from the land and have roots that should be nourished.

B Wright

## NIGHT

In any Hopi village the shadowed night is a time for conjuring, particularly when the kivas are lit during ceremonials. Lights flicker and dim from strange directions, shining vertically from the ground or bobbing like fireflies among the darkened shapes of the houses. Smoke rising from kiva chimneys drifts in shifting half-lit clouds through the streets. Vaguely human forms move from house to kiva, fading in and out of the smoke in abstract patterns.

B Wright

## THE HOPI SHADOW

The shadow of a Hopi is a familiar friendly personage that accompanies him day or night. It shares his problems so they are not as unendurable as if borne alone. In this instance, a young Hopi boy had stayed overlong at Hotevilla to watch a dance and had to return at night to his home in Oraibi. As he jogged along through the dark all of the terrors of the night moved in about him. As his panic grew he suddenly saw someone just ahead of him dropping down the far side of a ridge on the trail toward Oraibi. With the thought that they could travel together he ran to catch the individual, but as he came over the ridge the figure was already crossing the valley. Despite the fact that the boy was one of the best runners in Oraibi he could not catch up to the dark figure ahead. Each time as he ran harder he kept thinking who could it be that could outrun him; then as they rushed into the streets of Oraibi the dark form melted into the shadows and disappeared. Puzzled and vaguely worried the boy asked his father about the incident the next morning. His father smiled with amusement and explained, "It was your shadow. You didn't worry anymore about your fears of the dark, and he brought you home quickly and safely. Your shadow always helps you."

## THE POWAKA

The story of this encounter was related to me by a Hopi friend. As a youngster he was returning from the fields at dusk with a young friend. Slowly making their way up the mesa edge toward the town they noticed a large, black dog loping along toward the village. Since neither of them recognized the dog they began to throw rocks at it, and to escape this unwanted attention it fled into some ruined houses. The boys, caught up in the excitement, followed in hot pursuit until they succeeded in cornering the animal in a building with only one exit. They converged upon the opening and the friend darted inside first only to emerge immediately, pale and shaken and unable to speak. So my friend stepped into the doorway and found himself face to face not with a dog but with a man standing against the back wall with his blanket held in front of his face and no sign of the large black dog. It was a dreaded *powaka,* a two-hearted person or witch.

B. Wright

## THE SUN SNAKE

Long ago some people came to Shungopovi and asked if they could join that village. The chief, however, was loath to let them enter as they refused to lay down their weapons. Rather than letting them enter he told them to go a short distance to the west to Köngoivi and make their home. Very soon after settling there they were attacked by a monster that stole their children. This horrible creature appeared as a long thin snake with wings who seized stray children in its coils and flew off toward the Sun with them. The men who tried to overcome it would become entangled in its long tail that looped and twisted about them. In desperation the people returned to Shungopovi which again refused them entry and instead offered them land to the east. It is here that they still live but each year they return to offer prayer feathers against the return of the sun snake, *Tukchi-i*.

## MASWIK'CHINA

The Maswik'china represents the spirit of youth and the hoped-for fertility of the tribe. It is at one and the same time the forerunner of death and the embodiment of spring, harbinger of all crops. It represents the good and the beautiful of new life that can be achieved with the cooperation of Masau'u, the deity who controls the land. Without the presence of Masau'u the land would foster neither crops nor humans. It was considered good to have the Maswik'china appear in the villages to dance to the cicada-like music of the Hopi flutes and a sad day when they returned no more. Maswik'china is one of the many Hopi kachinas, and it shares a symbolic interpretation of springtime with several other kachinas.

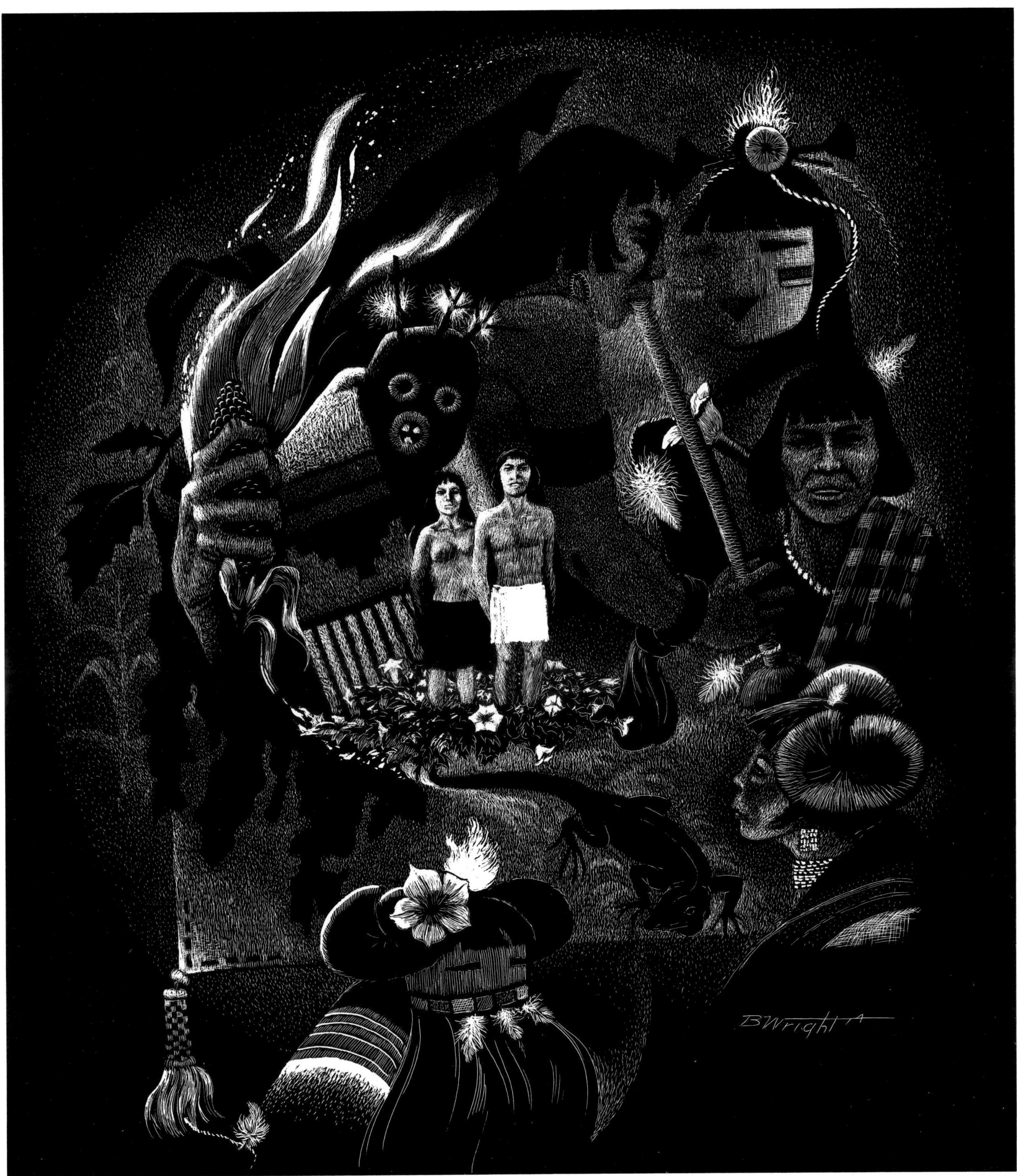
BWright

## THE ALOSAKUM

The Two Horned Society (The Alosakum) to which many Hopi men belong is one associated with hunting and game animals. The young men enter this society under the protection of Talatumsi, the deity known as Dawn Woman, who is the mother of all animals and who controls their movements. Occasionally as a man hunts alone she may appear to him as a young woman, often be-spattered with blood. But whoever sees her thus is forever after a luckier hunter. Symbolic of Talatumsi and her role among the animals is the helmet worn by members of the society replicating the two-horned heads of mountain sheep. She appears on altars in effigy, and countless shrines are devoted to her across not only Hopi land but other pueblo regions as well.

## MASAU'U

To the Hopis, the manifestations of Masau'u, one of their main deities, are many. These forms are interrelated through overlapping associations. Masau'u is the deity of the Underworld and by extension, death and darkness; for the Underworld is the antithesis of the bright living world of the Hopis. The Hopis, who emerged from this nether land, met their deity seated alone in the night by his fields warmed only by fires. He is then also the deity of fire. Because Masau'u can pass back and forth through the plane between the world of the living and the one of the dead, he is obviously the one who controls that plane, the earth. Those who walk on the land, plant crops on it or build villages pay homage to him. When they enter the kiva or the grave, they are in his domain. He is not, however, always a fearsome creature of the night for when he appears in the daytime he is the opposite in appearance and can only be distinguished from any other handsome, young Hopi man by the incredible length of his feet.

B. Wright

## THE PAHO

*Pahos* or prayer feathers are works of beauty compounded from elements of their environment by the Hopis. These bits of feathers and wood are as multitudinous as the prayers they carry to the supernaturals. From the cloud-like drifting down of the eagle to the water-seeking willow branch, each part of the prayer feather has involuted associations for the Hopis and their supernaturals. The *paho* is carefully and reverently placed where the spirit to whom it is addressed can see it and answer the heartfelt but unspoken prayer it carries.

BWright

# *Acknowledgments*

*The Unchanging Hopi* is about a people who have found a way to exist in a land of extremes which reluctantly shares food and shelter with any living beings. They respect and honor the Kachinas which provide them with the means of existence and atop the three stark mesas in Northeastern Arizona they live with dignity and joy. We wish to express our appreciation to the Hopi people, known and unknown.

We also wish to thank the collectors of Barton Wright's scratchboards who have kindly permitted us to reproduce them on these pages. The collectors are: Clay Lockett, Russell Nagle, Edward B. Danson, Don Dedera, Rex Howard, Tom Via and Eugene B. Adkins. Also Mrs. Barton Wright, Vivian Morales, Patrick Houlihan, Mr. and Mrs. David Cross, Mr. and Mrs. Paul Weaver and Mr. and Mrs. James K. Howard.

THE EDITOR

# *Selected Readings*


CRANE, LEO. *Indians of the Enchanted Desert.* Boston: Little, Brown & Co., 1925.

CURTIS, EDWARD S. *North American Indians,* Vols. 12, 16, 17. Norwood, Massachusetts, 1907–1930.

DOZIER, EDWARD P. *Hano: A Tewa Indian Community in Arizona.* New York: Holt, Rinehart & Winston, 1966.

NELSON, J. L. *Rhythm for Rain.* Boston: Houghton-Mifflin, 1937.

NEQUATEWA, EDMUND. *Truth of a Hopi.* Flagstaff, Arizona: Northland Press, 1973.

O'KANE, WALTER COLLINS. *The Hopis: Portrait of a Desert People.* Norman: University of Oklahoma Press, 1953.

QUOYAWAYMA, POLINGAISI. *No Turning Back.* Albuquerque: University of New Mexico Press, 1964.

TITIEV, MISCHA. *Old Oraibi: A Study of the Hopi Indians of Third Mesa.* Cambridge: Papers of the Peabody Museum of American Archaeology and Ethnology, Vol. 22, No. 1, Harvard University, 1944.

TYLER, HAMILTON A. *Pueblo Gods and Myths.* Norman: University of Oklahoma Press, 1964.

UDALL, LOUISE. *Me and Mine.* Tucson: University of Arizona Press, 1969.

WRIGHT, BARTON. *Kachinas: A Hopi Artist's Documentary.* Flagstaff, Arizona: Northland Press, 1973.

The Unchanging Hopi

was designed by Robert Jacobson

and set in Linotype Granjon and Garamond Display.

It was printed on Quintessence Dull

and bound at Roswell Bookbinding.